OTHER EDITIONS IN THIS SERIES

George Garrett, guest editor, *Best New Poets 2005*

Eric Pankey, guest editor, *Best New Poets 2006*

Natasha Trethewey, guest editor, *Best New Poets 2007*

Mark Strand, guest editor, *Best New Poets 2008*

Kim Addonizio, guest editor, *Best New Poets 2009*

Claudia Emerson, guest editor, *Best New Poets 2010*

D.A. Powell, guest editor, *Best New Poets 2011*

Matthew Dickman, guest editor, *Best New Poets 2012*

Best NEW Poets

2013

50 Poems from Emerging Writers

Guest Editor Brenda Shaughnessy

Series Editor Jazzy Danziger

Copyright © 2013 by the Rector and Board of Visitors of the University of Virginia

All rights reserved, including the right of reproduction in whole or in part in any form.

This book was published in cooperation with *Meridian* (readmeridian.org), Samovar Press, and the University of Virginia Press.

For additional information, visit us at
bestnewpoets.org
facebook.com/BestNewPoets
twitter.com/BestNewPoets

Cover design by Atomicdust | atomicdust.com

Text set in Adobe Garamond Pro and Bodoni

Printed by Thomson-Shore, Dexter, Michigan

ISBN 13: 978-0-9766296-8-9
ISSN: 1554-7019

Contents

About *Best New Poets*

Welcome to *Best New Poets 2013*, our ninth installment of fifty poems from emerging writers. In *Best New Poets*, the term "emerging writer" is defined as someone who has yet to publish a book-length collection of poetry. The goal of *Best New Poets* is to provide special encouragement and recognition to new poets, the many writing programs they attend, and the magazines that publish their work.

From February to April of 2013, *Best New Poets* accepted nominations from writing programs and magazines in the United States and Canada. Each magazine and program could nominate two writers, each of whom would be granted a free submission. For a small reading fee, writers who had not received nominations could submit two poems as part of our Open Competition, which ran from April 5 to May 25. Eligible poems were either unpublished or published after April 15, 2012.

In all, we received 1,985 submissions for a total of roughly 3,970 poems. Seven readers and the series editor blindly ranked these submissions, sending a few hundred selections to this year's guest editor, Brenda Shaughnessy, who chose the final fifty poems.

To learn more, visit us online at **bestnewpoets.org**, or follow us on Twitter (@ **BestNewPoets**) or Facebook (**facebook.com/BestNewPoets**).

Introduction

What could possibly be better than a *new poet?* Better, fresher, rarer than new shoes, new love, new worlds. All those other new things necessitate a *getting rid of* the old versions: they're worn through, trashed, gotten over, replaced. But new poets don't get rid of the old poets; they write through them, on top of them, around them, in honor of them, in spite of them, even in ignorance of them. New poets' books sit proudly on the top of a stack of old poets' books, hoping to one day be as dog-eared and well-thumbed and memorized as the oldies. Hoping to not be as forgotten, hoping to find new life through readers who immortalize. New poets' poems rib and jostle and compete with and tease and adore old poets' poems. And speak to, sing with, clang and jangle with each other's.

And there's the really interesting scene. The new poets are not just a new generation of scribblers born to Glückian and Ashberyish bloodlines, or of Cliftonic and Gilbertian culture. They are a hybrid cyborg technotopian many-headed gorgonian (those heads have snakes) galactic hive-made-entirely-of-queens-yet-the-work-gets-done mythic futuristic scary and reassuring swarm of wordsmiths.

This may sound a bit overstated, but I don't think by much.

I'm glad I'm not a new poet. I wouldn't be in this book if I were. The stuff new poets are writing now is stratosphuckingspheric, if I may coin a neologism. Poems in this selection do things like realign the essential quadratic relation between human bodies, god, nature and death: "Sky the color of poison, I prayed / with watertight lips" (Michael Simon's "Interstate"). These poems are not just made by new poets. They make new truths, new ontologies: "Black nights come / for everyone" (Aran Donovan's "two left feet") and "Under the interstate it's all musicbox. The boys live here / entirely" (Benjamin Sutton's "*from* Footnotes on the City") and "Desire lives on the tongue's tip" (Derek JG Williams's "Ode to the Tongue").

And, oh, don't they make of messes divine music? "I lived on a circle then moved onto a square, / Then wandered back into the kitchen half-drunk" (Amy Woolard's "A Girl Gets Sick of a Rose")—and here this new poet taps an old one for a leg up.

And sorrows sing bittersweet: "'I'm going to be a writer someday,' Ezra said, 'but not as my main job'" (Micah Chatterton's "Now, Someday").

I hope these new poets not only rejoice in their inclusion in this anthology, but allow themselves to be astonished by the company they are in. I hope the other new poets whose work I read also enjoy and respect the work of those who made the cut. For it really was a "cut"; it hurt me to select only 50 poems. There were *so many* good ones.

Something truly amazing is happening in literature lately. I don't know if it's because of increased connectivity, the constant practicing of writing on social media, the immediate gratification when everyone "likes" the finely-wrought status, or what, but the new poets are writing off the chain, their metaphors in 4-D, and their juxtapositions smashing cosmic distances, and their metrics and their rhymes and their formal skills like giant eggs of newborn baby spiders crawling everywhere. All of us, old poets and new poets alike, know these spiders bite. The poison is dizzying. The new generation of poets is writing killer poems, but the poems don't kill us—they only make us stronger.

—Brenda Shaughnessy
September 2013
Brooklyn, New York

The series editor wishes to acknowledge

Jeb Livingood

Molly Damm

Juliana Daugherty

Celeste Lipkes

Marielle Prince

Jocelyn Sears

Safiya Sinclair

Chelsey Weber

Jason Coleman

Emily Grandstaff

Atomicdust

Hannah Sanghee Park

BANG

Just what they said about the river:
rift and ever.

And nothing was left for the ether
there either.

And if anything below could mature:
A matter of nature.

It may have been holy as scripture
as scribes capture

meaning all that was there and only
(one and lonely)

is all that is left, and wholly
whose folly.

The sky bleached to cleanly
clear, evenly

to have left the world,
to what is left of it—

Could you have anything left to covet?
Covertly met: coverlet. Clover, bet. Come over *et*—

Javier Zamora

This Was the Field
after my father

What you've heard is probably true. Some say it's true—I haven't seen it—not here close to the coast. Doña Raquel says the islands are where bombs come from. She says those people are guerrilleros, that their dogs carry messages, and that their children are born with sickles up their asses. Teniente Milton says guerrilleros are scared of this town. What you've heard about Radio Venceremos is probably true. Last week, Milton broke four of Carlito's fingers. If it weren't for Carlito's mother swearing she would beat the shit out of him—I don't know—Milton dragged him to the middle of the street and pointed his M-16 at his forehead. This much is true. That Las Fuerzas will shoot kids for listening to that radio—I don't know—I haven't seen it—not here. It started early one morning—the helicopter flying low to the ground—this happened five days in a row—this was the field we played on—one shipment an hour. It was the first time a helicopter flew over our town. All we read and heard about were battles in Tecoluca, the islands, the capital, the volcanoes. I ran under the helicopter, it never landed—I don't know—it just threw bodies onto the field. Mamá Soccoro says guerrilleros might be winning. She says it's the beginning of the real war.

nominated by New York University

Anna Claire Hodge

Where We Have No Business
for Tarfia

Between the wig shop and milliner, the Ethiopian
restaurant, chairs long stacked on tables. Our mothers

imagine us like this: in a city bound by river, our wrists
bound by desperate fingers. They beg us, *stay in groups*

or better: *stay home.* Friend, so many nights, we strode
from bars, from warm homes onto sidewalks, giggled

as the toes of our boots caught on loose bricks, our hands
not poised on the triggers of mace, but threaded together,

warmer that way. Arms thick from the bright wool of our coats
in colors that blazed under street lamps: one purple, one red.

Like our lips: stained with wine or a new, slick gloss. Same crimson
as your wedding sari, the blood that never came. Or the silk in which

you wrapped me, oceans, airplanes ago in Bangladesh, when I came
to you broken, and brought you what I could: good bourbon, my hands

to slap mosquitoes or gesture wildly as I told you *what he did. What I
didn't.* Those mornings we slept and slept, despite the call to prayer

spilling like milk tea from the loudspeakers of the minarets,
despite the honking of impenetrable traffic below, the bleating of horns

constant, like the *slap slap* of sneakers on pavement in Richmond, as people
stronger than the dawn, stronger than you and I, rose to run a race for a cause

we weren't sure of: cancer, distended bellies. Hungry like a woman in her
        sheets, fists curling
and uncurling like blooms: beyond her windows, useless morning.

Chad Temples

Waking, Walking, Singing
after Morris Graves

Miniglyphs. Bended wings. A bird
bummed by the muteness of winter

getting bluesy in the dead cherry.
The TV's blue our companion moon.

Night bird. Night boy.
Tired of masturbating, I watch a monk

drench his robe in rainwater,
wrap himself and start to shiver.

As if the air were gunflint. As if a gel
pressed between some magician's thumbs.

A white smoke twists from him. The body is
a blameless thing. Birds sing.

This Russian stream is awfully illegal.
(Note: to move the mtn move the river.)

Claudia Burbank

TGIF

So here's Diana and her hounds, all toned and goddessy
sprawled around a table at McKibbin's
doing shots and chasers, the swing of the kitchen's
door at her back. It's the usual Friday odyssey—
minor gods and goddesses, satyrs, nymphs, and titans;
a buck (what a rack!) surrounded by some sirens.
The very buck, it happens, who only last week
gave Diana's nipple a tweak
in the hot tub, nibbles now a pair of naiads.
Easy shot, those gonads,
Diana, somewhat blotto, somewhat woozy,
muses as he snorts (here a hoof-stamp), snorts
at his own dumb joke and escorts
(smooth) a sprite toward the door. With a bluesy
beat Diana thumbs her bow—thumbs, thumbs, till she snaps
the string so violently it snaps
the dogs up, quivering, freezes mid-swing
the kitchen door, every faun and gorgon scrambling.
All neck and haunch, magnificent,
the stag stands still, feels a bead
drip where Diana draws a bead, feels the spent
arrow of her eyes and the speed
of hounds at his flank as (not one to diddle)
he flicks and bounds McKibbin's Bar & Griddle.

Darin Ciccotelli

Superpower

I thought
telepathy was
just a way of
pining, of
ascertaining which
teenager had
her sexual
ipswitch set on
yes. I thought
invisibility was
for lingering in
bedrooms.
If you suddenly
can turn into a
muscular
freak, or if by
awry experiment you
are made muscular
freak, or if
you own
technologically superior
vestments that
duplicate the torso
of said muscular

freak, then
whatever punishments the
day exacts on
you can be
revised. The sun's
permanence can
be toppled. Lying down
in backyard clover
isn't nearly as
idyllic as anyone they
named an
elementary school after
ever suggested. It
leaves that
chemical burn on
your knees. It
necessitates panic.
I wonder if you can
tolerate hearing
about how
much better it all
is now. An
unusual amount of
cardamom is
kept in my
house. I have people
who know what
to do with
that. Sure, the almost
flammable jelly
of the grass

distempers
the skin. All I have
to do to entertain
someone is
fill up her
inflatable pool,
let her tote
water around and
occasionally
protest the
extermination
of snails. I can
make her
crumple with
laughter if
I feign
death. I mean,
I've been to Russia.
I've seen permanent
sun, white like
a horse's
muzzle. I've seen
how much ice
cream those
people eat. If
you've anticipated
that previous
versions of me would
dislike the most
recent version
you're sort of

a killjoy. I've
designed my whole
life to
please people
like you. What I've
said under my breath
is that the
sun abides
even our irritability.
I don't have
a body, I have
the meteor
forthcoming,
the problem that
I'm not talking
about. If
you calibrate
between inspired
worry and the
other thing
I'll be happy
to reset
the instruments.
But I'm going
to go
home first and
pretend to be
afraid of
my daughter. It
pleases her.

Peter Mishler

Fludde

The light had its gradient pull.
I scanned away from the schoolyard
with the lens sparkling. And the moon
divvied up into separate grains.
I find the coin I'd skimmed
from the lake, and when it cries,
I'm reminded: the lead ocean itself
is waiting, with love, within us.
None of us dared trim away
the snake's skin that summer for fear
of what was beneath its unwinding.
Beyond us, all of our glassware
is being sown over in a future
where a shoulder blade is found
and dug up again. It will know
nothing of us, or the ocean
that crept through the sun. Difficult
child, shrilling lake unhinged,
you stand in a state of mild yawning
in a church of your own gold
peeling your shadow from
the diving board. On stage!
it was said. File in! The sounds
of undressing and song coursed through

the back halls, then were lost behind
the beverage machines. We were placed
in line as if meant to return
our crossbows. And I loved these
cross-purposes. At night,
in our beds, our legs snapped like dawn
on a hinterland of ice.
We were told God was winnowing us
into fascinating lutes.
While the flood ranged southward.

Brian Tierney

Jawbone

> Of people the air only
> Remembers a few odd syllables.
> It rehearses them moaningly:
> Black stone, black stone.
> *Plath*

We feed our father to the ground again
this night: my brother & I take turns

with the tumbril & shovel, shackled
inmates shadowed by no moon or clock,

our pink hands lifting saw-toothed dark
in clumps, as if ripping meat

from the bone-yard, our pink hands
like figurines', & near-night filling, to the lip,

its glass of water & bourbon hot as blood
in the chalice of a rabbit neck

we keep by the corpse as our sacrifice—
by trinkets of inverse pillow-magic:

canaries broken into fine powder,
& salted cock feet, & slack string, gin-

soaked feathers, the jawbone of an ass
we whet to clear webs from Dad's eyes—

to shave his gray head so finches won't
make their West-African headache nest.

*What is sweeter than honey, what's stronger
than lions?* we sing, not wanting answers

really: we-the-righteous who raise heroic feats
along the Sorek Valley in our mind

this night: every dead dirt lump set aside
with our good shoes like kisses from childhood,

our toes cut, & what's inside us going
back to the earth when we raise him

in the way of ants hoarding food for the living
who must believe that the sun plays

dead, too—that sorrows of beehives
are relieved by mighty gestures of renewal,

though I say to Sean *We don't have to
cry just because we're supposed to...*

And when it's done, & we ring & ring
with the harrowed faith of bent-over slaves,

the stone pace of a Greek chorus—
What is sweeter than honey? Not answering...

a dying fox enters dusk's haloed fringe
saying *Water, water—give the hunted*

water—& I say *No, death is mine, tonight, to give,*
may you enter thirsty like the bearded men

in our Tierney's Tavern photos: men digging
at what's hard, carving coal seams, carrying

black dust in their lungs all their soot-black
lives: a blackness, inside, we are made of.

Benjamin Sutton

from *Footnotes on the City*

To honor each building, a boy is named in the just after. A name

& a name until the city is more child

than city. Under the interstate it's all musicbox. The boys live here

entirely. They are as much excavation as they are elbows

& collarbones. After the first fire ate the city

the fire built it back bigger than ever

The boys sleeptalk the night into the shape of skyline. Sleeptalk the air

into the touch of thighs. They are under the misunderstanding

if they think hard enough they can bring a bridge into existence

A never-ending steeple. A cathedral built around

a cathedral. They think they can find the mother

to the motherland

Michael Simon

Interstate

Children have a blueness all their own
audible in the dark as a torch
in a sepulchre. Alone in belted pants
my betters gave me, I too thought
immersion was the favored means of language
interrogation. First your ears and friends,
and then you take off your clothes. Notice the scar
tissue forming on the verb *to be*. The letter
I, proud as a prison tower, stands
a bit shorter in the rain. And the walls
of your mouth are slippery—hard to get a foothold
in—when you go under like Houdini
in a locked barrel blundering downstream.
Words to heal the world's infernal fissures—
yeah, right. This was the year of the skiff
surfing the clouds, while below a cop
checked under my father's hood, patted his thighs,
and overlooked the sack of cottonmouth heads
in the trunk. Sky the color of poison, I prayed
with watertight lips. Later my father
explained the game—some red ribbon,
a flashlight, the spine of a grouper laid out
in the grass—to be played in the velvet
scarcity, and I was the only rule, he said,
the only one worth ruling.

Stephanie Rogers

How It Kept On

My niece says that, when she grows up,
she wants to turn all the animals into rocks.
Three years old: already she pretends
to pull cicadas from her hair, hold them
on her tongue, and let them scream.
Someone told me once that children learn
to imitate our disarray. As a kid I used to
wonder what it would be like to go
from worn-in corduroys to all dolled up
in a dress, exposing nothing but a sliver
of clavicle. In Brooklyn now, at 29,
instead I watch the sun go down, pretend
the clouds explode into a flock of red
high heels descending. A man professed
on the train today that Jesus rides a UFO
to Earth and whispers to me while I sleep.
In that moment, I recalled the night
I watched my father use a spoon to crush
a pill, then sniff the powder off my history
book, how the world grew stranger then,
and afterward, how it kept on.

Josh Kalscheur

Katari

After hours of strict respect
from the man who loves me
for a time each year, I enter
the cookhouse with a mirror
and a shard of louver
to loosen two teeth of a turtleshell comb
from my forehead.
It was a gift to me, the comb.
The skilled threadwork left me
leaning. The respect that ran for me
now runs from me and I lay
down my arms. From a line
by the road a hanging skirt drifts
upward. I was not always loved
so heavily, so accepted
into the rhythm of survival,
so stalled in a bloodline
which bends for no one,
not even the beautiful.
In the right darkness, I go
to the top of the hill
where Americans listen to all
the sounds the ocean
never makes. I want to clean them

from their happiness until the flies
gather where fruit splits
its sweetness. I want my shore
to teach them the smallness
of a flower grove, a shadow
which sways into the water
and lessens.

Cori A. Winrock

Débridement

When I find out I'm pregnant I bury my wedding dress
in the front yard—letting everyone in the neighborhood watch me

peel the blue satin over my head: my slipless figure & a shovel.
The school bus slowing its yellow dredge to witness the anxiety

of the uncovered. I dig a tunnel to my grandmother straight through
my mother—her old flowerbulbs empty rattles, their bodies now fists

in earth. I lick my ungloved hands & gather fragments of bone & leftover
teeth into my mouth. How else to feed the matryoshkaed body, its double

hummingbird hearts? Ashes. Ashes. In the tunnel I uncover a nightgown
I sloughed off as I lost my virginity to a song about elevens; crawl back into

its florals & incorporeal sense of expectation—the assistant's glittering self
sawed open to applause. Down here my new cluster of cells can't echo or mirror.

It lullabies me with replication. Tells me to revisit the rooms I flooded
just to peel off the wallpaper, to uproot the ugly azaleas from the family

before & before. When I arrive at my childhood I undress
the house like a wound.

Rochelle Hurt

Poem in Which I Play the Runaway

It could open with a party, strewn
with girls like tinsel, girls looking
for a house to stuff themselves in, girls
with two parents, girls glaring
with the joy of needlessness.

Or a chase scene: the snagged walls
of the Dallas house like a mother's dress,
long-emptied of men, and closing on me.

I never wanted a home in him,
but the sex was like licking sheets
of corrugated iron, torn maw breathing
the corrosion in, the scent of him alone
like coming into a father's midnight grip.

In this way, I was forever
the runaway, indolent trinket of his.

But if you want it, I'll give
the story of a woman's deboning
by a pair of junk-rutted hands,

her good marrow honed to a prick
on the butt of a shotgun.

And how she loved it, the sin itself
a kind of homelessness.

Kyeren Regehr

Eversion

> "...what they call passion is not some emotional energy, just the friction between their souls and the outside world."
> *from Andrei Tarkovky's film* Stalker

I want to be exiled from choice. The which-which-itch of my six-fingered soul. I want my passion to be singular. A molten sphere ballooning in light, my glassblowers' lips exhaling...

It used to be simpler: before babymania, that milk-sweet swell—kiss them, kiss them, cherub cuisine. I want to be exiled from miscellanea. Humdrum haven of home, hoovering me inside-out. I want to get out

of my open-flame mind, that synaptic sandpaper smelt—relationships rub us smooth, raw. Give me a dirt-footed baptism, house of rain, rucksack of storms. I want a message in the gravel. I'll scrawl one myself, soul-shaped, winged. Wind-smitten. Lift me frictionless, lift me out of my fountainhead, carry me

back to the ground. I want to fall fail fuck it all up, till there's nothing else I want.

Mikko Harvey

Cannonball

I heard it was my turn to be shot from the cannon. At first
I didn't believe it. People are always joking about these things.
My friends told me it was serious this time though. Apparently
there was a whole meeting about it, and people were divided
on the issue. At the meeting, an old man took the microphone.
No one had seen him in years, but he showed up to this meeting
because he felt strongly that I should be shot from the cannon.
His argument was so graceful, apparently, everyone in the audience
was crying. His conclusion was about how hard the times
were becoming, how the cannon stood for human resilience,
and how I stood for all humans. In a sense, by shooting me
from the cannon they were shooting themselves up too.
I was simply the spokesperson. And what an honor it was
to be the spokesperson, to carry the weight of the whole human
family on my skinny shoulders. Fuck, I thought to myself. I always
knew metaphors would be my downfall. "I am flattered," I said
to my friend Amy. "I understand this is quite an honor. But
why do I have to be shot from the cannon? I would rather
do some community service, maybe even give a speech."
I am quite anxious about public speaking, so you can tell
how serious this was to me. I was not looking forward to being
shot from the cannon at all. For one thing, no one who had been
shot from the cannon had come back to say how it went.
"Don't worry," Amy said. "There is probably a place over

the hill that's better than this shitty city. That's probably
where you're going. Plus," she said, "I hear the air is like
a blanket when you're in it. People are so afraid of falling
they don't enjoy the flying, but the truth is they're the same."
"Wow," I said. I was slightly offended that Amy had used
my impending doom to generalize about human fear and
happiness. I didn't have time for that. Still, she made me
feel better about the whole thing, especially the part about
this shitty city. It was, after all, not the best place to be and
the cannon was a way out. So I started walking, and every time
I passed a car, I thought to myself, I love you car, this is the end. Then
I approached the receptionist at the government building. She was
licking her lips, seductively I thought, though they may have been
just chapped. I cleared my throat and said, "I'm ready." She
looked up at me and suddenly I regretted everything. I grabbed
her face and kissed her. "Oh," she said. "Thank you," she said.
"I'll tell my boss to build a cannon. We didn't think you'd come."

nominated by Ohio State University

Emily Van Kley

Physical Education

The day Coach set up his camera
you were running hurdles

in the upstairs hallway (the track
outside waned to gravel at 50 meters

and could not be trusted to balance
such spindly structures, nor to cleanly

launch a trackshoe's elegant sole).
Coach meant film to expose

firsthand the mistakes he said you
were always making: the arm's

drift out of square while erupting
legs and abdomen up from the blocks,

the foot unpointed at lift,
the extra inch of air between plank

and crotch. Transgressions
unfelt by the body pouring fast

across linoleum, breathing up
over wood and steel obstacles,

1, 2, 3, racheting to a halt
before brick wall at hallway's end.

Strictly speaking, the camera
was a good idea. Except

that you noticed nothing
of stride or armstroke

when Coach fed tape
into player. Instead

the unexpected grace
of your breasts

lifting and falling
in slow motion, unchained

to the muscle and bone
of the chest toiling behind.

Those insignificant pauses
in the body's line upward, scorned

by boys your age, unable to bolster
the puckered tube top purchased

on sale in anticipation of summer.
Inconsequential, and yet

plain excess to the body's utility,
the face blank as an elbow,

jaw a gear set tight for speed.
Those breasts lashed together

under the sportsbra's softshell,
floating up and settling back

as if gravity were to be
indulged on occasion,

a little pleasure. Speechless
when Coach asked *what did you see.*

Amy Woolard

A Girl Gets Sick of a Rose

When I asked for a pencil, they gave me a rattle.
When I asked for a hammer, they gave me a kiss.
All mongrel, no matter, I'll stay out past dinner;
I've practiced the answers to all of their tests.

I've given up sweets, their ridiculous shapes,
Their instructions on which ones have cherries.
Everything under the sun is lukewarm;
The poppies are blooming with worry.

When they gave me a map, I thought they were done,
I thought I could take off my dress.
They told me one town was as good as another,
Sent me packing, all fiddle, no case.

Each cul-de-sac greyed like a cooled blown bulb.
All dashboard, all driver, all sky & no cake.
Each neighborhood gatehouse, a live empty socket;
When they asked for my ticket, I gave them a wink.

The instructions all listed Step One as Repeat.
The poppies were planted in rows at the park.
I lived on a circle, then moved onto a square,
Then wandered back into the kitchen half-drunk.

The screen door, the scrim, the latch, the last word.
The glass throats of each vase open wide.
A house is the largest tombstone we make;
We keep walking, grateful, inside.

nominated by Smartish Pace

Tarfia Faizullah

Self-Portrait as Slinky

It's true I wanted
        to be beautiful before
                authentic. Say the word
                        exotic. Say minority—
a coiled, dark curl
        a finger might wrap
                itself in—the long
                        staircase, and I was
the momentum
        of metal springs
                descending down
                        & down—say tension.
The long staircase,
        and I was a stacked series
                of spheres fingertipped
                        again into motion—say
taut, like a child
        who must please her
                parents but doesn't
                        know how—a curl pulled
thin—I wanted to be
        a reckoning, to gather
                into each day's pale
                        hands—that helpless

lurching forward
　　　in the dark—another
　　　　　soaked black ringlet,
　　　　　　　that sudden halting—

Michelle Bonczek

Entering the Body
after Gunther von Hagen's Body Worlds

All I could think of at first
was cooking. Of that skinned

rabbit in my freezer, fur torn, gaze
jammed between a package of phyllo

and a carton of ice cream.
Of all that succulent meat

dripping from its own skeleton,
sweet marrow and a bottle of merlot, but

even here
I end up in the palace of longing.

Caught in the arms of no arms.
Trying to bend a body

to my own. A skeleton
follows its muscled canvas

and I long
to be inside one, to hold
the other.

But you can't translate flesh.

Not with polymer, nor contemplation,
not even with a prolonged hand

shake or make out session.
Not in the slow unbuttoning

of a wine-stained blouse or in the stripping
of tendon from bone, muscle filleted

into C-section, pelvis cavity unsewn.
In this case, a uterus

the size of a thumb. Inside me, one jabs
like an eyelash in the heavens (yes,

the heavens). Here in this museum,
two blue eyes drift from two halves

of a severed head. How long do we stare
into mirrors. So long, I know,

my eyes roll
from their pockets till they bump
my tiny

tiny ossicles dripping notes
into my ears, *not yet*
not yet.

But flesh will not wait.
I want to wrap my arms around this

sculpture's waist and ask him, *anything?*
Nuzzle my chin in the meat-cleave

of his shoulder. Play my fingers
over his bones, over his exposed

vertebrae like a vibraphone.
Lick his neck until his brain coral

flowers.

Meighan L. Sharp

Beyond Measure

No elegant beginnings for me. It's February
and down the street a Christmas wreath
clings to brick siding. I'm riding out

beginnings—bruised chest & belly. A February
countdown to chemo cocktails. Steri-strips
cling to my skin's incisions like dirty siding—I'm riding out
this need to be chipper, the way I must

count days since diagnosis, repeat my birth date, strip
my body for surgeons who shake hands, make jokes,
snip away muscle and submucosa. I must
please, be a good sport, when in Versed haze I think

my body should be circled by surgeons who hold their hands
at my perimeter and chant *light as a feather* until
I levitate like a good sport at a slumber party. I think
if some animal, huge and mute, appeared

at the perimeter of the post-op hallway and lifted me, light as a feather,
I might be cured. I'd sleep in one of its arms while the other
batted away mute scalpels and earnest third-year residents. Claws would appear
to shred IV bags, frighten phlebotomists. Sound asleep, I'd know nothing.

I might be cured, curled in the matted fur of its arms.
My scarred skin falls away like dirty snow, a dropped wreath
as the beast lurches to the woods. Sound asleep, I know nothing
but the elegant measure of its breath.

Melissa Barrett

The Invention of the Metal Detector

My desire was a dark horse, a monolith—simultaneously fraught with guilt,
        shrill-eyed
And spinning like the mica in a marble shooter. I was tired: I would deign

To shut my eyes once my eyes finally shut. And yet my sleeping was
        pregnant with intent—

In a shrinking chapel, a bismuth mine, in glades that chattered though
        a citharist lulled us,
Wrens tumbled their way through turgid sails. Soapberries

Dripped from the boughs in wanderlust. Dripped in pink waxen shadows,
        your breath amaranthine, mine

Tagged with kite-strings. Bluebells shimmered up, lovestruck—
        the shad bushes pressed till
Dimension was gone. And the lianas, thieving across

The trunks, became quite at home. Today at Beinn Bhreagh, I woke up
Sucking on a tooth—a screw. No, on a net of woven steel wires.

Lisa Allen Ortiz

Confection
for Julie Mehretu

It rained last night. Three black birds walk
in the folds of her sheets: sticks and lines.
What a dream to wake up so close
to an imagined sea—the beach, the wharf, a blanket of fog,
lines, lines, eraser marks. Imagine wind. What does wind
feel. When wind wakes. *Come close*
she tells her lover, her imagined lover,
her own black legs, long spider legs,
marks, marks. Cut: this is a cityscape. Slice, dice: this
is what I mean by rain. We're all in it together.
When you wake in the morning you emerge from my body
birthed from the electric storm in the desert
outside the city where I was born. Give me a pencil.
I'll draw you a map.

Laura Passin

The Egon Schiele Art Centrum, Český Krumlov

Women resent him,
or he draws them as if they do—
eyes bored and angry,

slumped spines opening
to grimly spread legs.
Or those heads, elaborately etched,

nearly breathing on the page,
disembodied—
torsos leaking

into an uncertain stream,
disappearing.
No context for nakedness:

each figure suspended
on blank ground, stripped of meaning
apart from Schiele's lust.

The self-portrait's plaque tells you
he was my age when he died.
His work still controlled

   by the lewd solipsism
of the very young:
   hunger to consume

each body we see,
   furious at the world's refusal
to be possessed.

I'll draw you a different scene.
   Yesterday I hid in a tea house
from a rain so determined

   it beat my red shoes pink.
A man paced near me,
   drenched, seething,

black hair forked and dripping
   down his forehead, fingers twisting
in relentless anger,

chilled as a drowned man
   —enraged and so contained
I couldn't help but want

   to mouth the clenched tendons
of his neck, palm
   his rigid shoulder,

close the few, endless feet
      between my gaze
and his body. And look,

      even now, see how I draw him:
all sex and no story,
      refusing to give back,

even in my own words too distant,
      so resentful I must set down the pen,
let the white background speak.

Gloria Muñoz

Your Biome Has Found You

And who will kiss open
the spine of the resurrection fern
that's hunched like a widow, hunched
like a shamed child? How it locks and hides
and browns under the sun—a laborer's
hands picking blistered tomatoes,
or a pile of bones, perhaps bird bones
—small, dry, silent.

              Here is the damp and thickest marsh
              of your interior wetland. And here,
              begins your tundra of moss, rock and shrub.
              Here is the thing you lost,
              perhaps the saddest or loveliest thing
              —remember? It was suddenly taken—as a fish
              spine is plucked from its open body on a plate.

And who will pry apart the arms
of the praying mantis who preys on her
lover? Who will resuscitate the tiny
bird whose head rests on a fallen nest? You
are helpless and wild here. A murmuration
of starlings pulses in your chest. A soundtrack
of breeding amphibians seeps through you. Cicadas
scream petrified from tree tops. The feral sounds
of wilderness sharpen your teeth.

It is November, goldfish scales crunch
under your soles, the autumnal scent
of a fire inhales you,
the aerials are coming and going.
While adding up all the dead things you carry,
you realize, there is so much dirt in you.
Still, your nautilus ears listen, waiting
to hear your native sea.

nominated by the University of South Florida

L.J. Sysko

Just try

to crop out anachronisms—.

Power lines unzip your sunset
no matter how you wade

like an egret through
the salt marsh, bending at the waist,

primordial fronds and velvet
bulrushes smacking past your ears.

The camera's dumb eye captures
what we ask it to, entombing it

within its geometry.
In Photography 101,

my improbable pomegranate dusks
wouldn't reconcile

with what swam out of the developer's bath.
Where are Van Gogh's rollicking clouds?

Magritte's black and blue hour?
My aftermath is so 4" x 6".

The fault is mine.
I'm sure of it. It's the way we talk

without looking at each other.
It's the way I struggle

against anger. It's the way our heroes slow
and sicken. It's the way it's presented

in the news. There's so much to be sad about.
I'd rather look away. But I'm telling myself

to be careful. Be careful about disparity,
about contrast, about separation. I'm saying

no to the phone gripped assiduously
in doctors' waiting rooms. In the chairs

someone's lined up like boats in a marina,
I force my eyes up to ask

an old question: why should I be
a me, a fisherman, or anyone? We leave

fingerprints on our photos, our screens,
the sliding windows that divide us.

I park my car—idle with its
hazards on, hood half in the cattails,

pointing to the scallop boats' dock, where
men smoke and gather, laughing,

acting cavalier like bored knights,
steering fork lifts one-handed,

piling ice chests for tonight's deep sea
charter. Even if the power plant's reactors

pepper my horizon, I wade deeper
for a picture. A Herring Gull

drops a Blue Crab, then lands
to peck its pale underbelly open.

Feathers and shell white as the sky,
sure as the tide, invite more gulls to land.

Their eyes blink
and blink in time with mine.

Lo Kwa Mei-en

Romance in Which Open Season Changes Everything

From garden to gauntlet in the year of what comes next.
    From ugly to ugly and armed. That hunt. One hot vex.

Babe of the break, a record heat, and I the dirty of honey
    of a wasp honed. One way to live under sun or money

is to break, baby. That bone. Love like how a wasteland
    welcomes back. Like to eat alive and start with the hand

you asked for. Love like from summer to summer to no
    land like the land that rises to meet my spine and throw.

My terror my weather again. A blond streak in the air
    and two thumbs of wing rapt in a fist of winter where

wants are wolves and what was sweeter this way stalks.
    Look, we last for days. But my rose to hip ratio talks

a good game over. I'd wild you over. I'd go down milk,
    the way you talk on two feet. You, full buck. That sulk,

from heart to hart in the year of coming down. Heart,
    I like to put a singing shaft through you. The good part,

a flesh to flash. A fence we go down fools for from top
    to touch. That tail. My turn. From the beg to the stop.

Anna Maria Hong

Four Barrels, Jaw & Locket

I was erased as a morning face
and slim as a pocket. I was steady
as dust and feathers blown hard across
a mackerel lake. I was bloody

chuffed in three-quarters, but I wasn't empty
anymore. I was tone, pause, energy.
I was a good stiff pour. Come and tempt me,
mimetic. Come shine on all fours. Urge me

untoward. A Maker made to tell. The day
began as terminal and ended so
right. How I wanted to be the only.
I did not want another to

replace my mine. No, I did not enjoy
"the process" of effacement, though it was a start.

nominated by Unsplendid

Max Somers

The Narrative Poem

The song and the words. Song and the long, kinked kink it makes to us in a line of years. Song not sentence. Song with all silences. Song singing its own song without us. Just a ringing. A tickle. Trickle. A little bucking song. Then, self bucking itself into song. Song need no, get no, no meaning. Song like tongue. New tongue. Song of the big tongue alone, alive, rolling. Wet song of our black bowels. For leaving, a song, a lovely. And all the lonely songs. And the gang of songs in question. This song was once a clean white dress. The be good song. Song through trouble right here in River City. We're coming to it. Fists in song, boots that keep breaking into. Echo songs. The mountain blows its head off giving song to the valley. Amaryllis plays the D scale sadly. Harold spies Marion's breasts. Marion looks away madly. Half-sung songs get hung-up inside. Songs make a mess of our willing, kinked bodies. Song then song gone. The song that sweats and slips. Song heat on the soles of our feet. Or buried song, not yet cold, cooling, cool. Shovel. Do it. Shovel on the song.

Derek JG Williams

Ode to the Tongue

Drawbridge sewn to jawbone.
Axe handle. Diviner of speech.

Median muscle. Axis muscle.
Taste-maker.

Fibrous changeling.
Backyard conjurer.

The silver tongue coaxes.
The fork tongue seduces.

The tongue twister teases.
And the tongue tied twitter.

Pierced treasure.
Silver pearl supine in its center.

Secret keeper. Crass eel.
Tamer of sweet breath.

Collector of sweat.
Desire lives on the tongue's tip.

A goliath.

John James

Chthonic

My light bulb is gone.
        It was dying anyways.
The room goes dark
        before I sleep. I lie
eyes closed, listening,
        hoping the radio waves
cause only one type
        of sick. My bed's
not safe. The feathers
        in my pillow came
from a factory in Beijing.
        Their birds fly east
in the shape of a *V.*
        On the edge where
my mother sat reading
        a bright picture book
something has taken
        her place. My father's
mouth, which I lost
        years ago, speaks
from a jar on the shelf.
        I ask my mother
what she did with the light.
        She says it's

under the bed. I ask
    my father why
he can't hear. He tells
    me he's underground.

Justin Runge

History

Here is what I've collected: He set fire to the front lawn. She learned and then forgot the guitar. Like all daughters, she was a vegetarian. He was sent to school on the mountain. She would run through the mountain. Their siblings stood in the way. The mountain was beautiful but merciless. Its trees loomed like chaperones. He took to botany. She slept in the haunted room. After the growth spurt, he was a natural athlete. She worked at a fast food restaurant. Both left without diplomas. He sat in a bunker, catching moths. She would walk to a payphone in the center of town. They would solve crossword puzzles days late. He escaped on a motorcycle, as in his favorite songs. They married on her birthday. Her hair was never longer. She left a home imploding. He had a television and a frying pan. They made mistakes—pepper oil, poison ivy. They had one child, then me.

Sarah Levine

Birds are Loosely Folded Napkins Thrown Into the Sky

1

It is summer and I am bleeding because I am in love with my knife holding hand and a constellation of carrots thrown on the table in the kitchen where you kissed me yesterday.

On the throat, nose, and tooth. The one I chipped while flying out of the tallest tree, trying to follow a white-necked bird back into the sky.

It was so easy. The flying that felt like running, running faster than I ever have; and I forgot how easy it made my heart burn like yolk on skillet until I kissed you yesterday.

Made my blood, a road of silk red handkerchiefs, stretch and sing and burn.

2

Do you remember the fire in the field
The one we started with match and wheat.

The way the wheat fell
While the earth went red.

Your sweat smelled afraid
And all I wanted to do was dance—

Spit into my hands
Shine my shoes

Dance like a flaming field.
You had to carry me out of there.

And I am not sorry
For the saddest magic I ever made.

Andrew C. Gottlieb

Portrait: Parsing My Wife As Lookout Creek

My wife sits, wipes, stands, zips, forgets to flush.
                                        Rushing,
the river's every agenda. We pull at our clothing,
    all day, humans, us,
                        all of us.
                            Try not to touch it.

I stand at the mirror, tuck a tail, a tag, tug a collar, flinch.
    What face is that?
                    Dry
outside, there are pines pushing against every reflecting sky
    in their own grim time.

My mother, tough one, British stiff.   *Sit up straight.   Excuse
    you.   That's a dessert spoon.*
                            Butler's fool,
ambassador for a childhood of rules.   One tough one.

Language gets us in its grip with its little links and latches,
    clasps, clamps,
                padlocks,
                        and we're lost: grappling.

Close your mouth when you chew.

In these river days,
what floats for me to find is the tissue, wet, a red filmy swirl
    the symptom of a drifting of cells
                        alluvial shift
in a body I know.

            Do you imagine first the conifer leaves?
Or the buried thread-like roots
    deeply reaching for food?
                    Plunging to touch the hidden skin
of the river.
            Dawn's lazy diffusion of hues lights the children's
confusion, their breakfast food,
                    flow
                            of this river that spews
stripped trunks, a shoe, crescent crust of dead everything,
    the ongoing plunge of innard and corpse.

Even my stepdaughter laughs, who for now laughs last,
                            least.
There's nothing funny about PMS: period.
                        My wife,
sure, she blushes, but it's love like the cat's torn mouse,
    the breast-split wren,
                the rejected owl pellet,
                            her kind of love,

the river's necessary way of sharing of what she's composed,
    unburdened by grammars, maps, latitudes, rules,
banks.

I am wading
    the lava rock and free-stone bed,

the old-growth bole
    wedged
        and lecturing only by collecting
every drifting thing that the muscle spits up, aggregate of flow,
  motion of bundling,
clustered abundance of the rushing's best refuse.
            I steady my step,

pocket a bottle, sift the river with my fingers, sink
  into its stunning flood,
       touch her every part.

Meg Day

Taker of the Temperature, Keeper of the Hope Chest
a sestina for Samyahsattva

Some have children in more foreseeable ways:
Cesareans, episiotomies, long hours of labor
or paperwork, adoptions that often take years.
My girl, she came to me when the rope burns
on my brother's neck were still fresh from his hanging,
the noose tied up in the knots of her mother's

tourniquet, needles still cluttering the floor. Mothers,
I've been told, are not born but made—always
runners of the tight shift, leavers of the light on—hanging
one hat up only to put on another, their labor
of love still & always labor. What candle burns
at both ends & lasts the night? We did not have years

to find our rhythm; we did not have yesteryears
to lean on or call up, nor succor, neither of us mothers
to phone with a thermometer in one cheek & the burns
of death's whiplash on the other. Some lose children in conceivable ways:
bee stings, enlistment, the bloody shock of difficult labor
that comes months too early & leaves every head hanging

in the waiting room. My girl made her great escape from a car hanging
upside-down over a freeway divider, all twelve of her years

broken into as many pieces, a puzzle of bone no surgeon's labor
could solve. Sorrow, I have learned, is long-legged like our mothers,
& stalks me with a glacier's patience. It sits in wait. If there are ways
of burying a body—still breastless & birdlike & fresh with sunburns—

no mother ever taught me how. If there is grief so torrid it burns
the mother out of you, I have known it. Her coat is still hanging
in the hall closet as if she, too, returns home with us on the subway
after stacking stones to sit by the window & stare. Years
ago, I dreamt she had broke free of the soil, face—like her mother's—
pale as a bar of soap. She padded into the kitchen to belabor

the leaky sink: its quiet drip that refuses the plumber's labor
& remains, like a stray dog at the door. Sometimes the sound burns
like sun through a magnifying glass into the middle of my mother-
less dreams, tapping at the ache found pregnant & hanging
between the ticking second hand of the mantle clock. Years
of sometimes have made me cautious of bus stops & railways

& other laborious intersections of bodies & speed. Unchanging
now, like my own mother, I am afraid of sleep. Instead, I layaway
& awake in the burn of night, my womb a bed no one's slept in for years.

Jennifer Givhan

Karaoke Night at the Asylum

When I was eleven, my mother sang karaoke
at the asylum. For family night, she'd chosen

Billie Holiday, & while she sang
my brother, a fretted possum, clung

to me near the punch bowl. I remember
Mother then, already coffin-legged—

mustard grease on her plain dress,
the cattails of her hair thwapping along

with the beat. The balding headstones
of the others—quarantined from

their own mothers and sisters and daughters—
I wondered if like us, they too were strange

alloys of sadness & forgetting
the words to the songs. I was a grave-

digger then. A rat fleeing ship. Mother,
who hadn't sung to me since I was a baby &

never again, was the lynchpin—
I'm still turning & turning the screw.

Jason Macey

Love Song for Cesar Vallejo

You, Cesar Vallejo, can go to hell.
The prisons in your eyes never
give way to ladies with parasols, and
my ears ring with the clanging
of you monotonously slamming the cells closed.

I, too, am reminded of my death
every day of my life,
growing weary of the cost of
printing pages of sad poetry,
stung eternally by Existence's hornets, but I,
unlike you, Cesar Vallejo,
would suffer this exodus privately.

Somewhere, Cesar Vallejo, a guitar plays while
a girl with skin like moonlight
dances and sings. Her voice is
like a crow's, but,
because she is beautiful, we
blend her voice with
the voices of angels we
imagine she hears.

Somewhere, I find you writing
poems about yourself. I imagine

you sitting, perhaps, at
the side table in a Parisian cafe.
Because you are mine, I
imagine that I suffer with you.
Goddamn you, Cesar Vallejo.
Goddamn you, brother.

Scott Miles

Ode to the Gods of French Cinema

In Rousseau's *Between the Rain*,
the leading man's a stepped-on sandwich
every time the starlet
turns her back to pour
her naked body into her crumpled dress.
So the world's a place that doesn't need our eyes
to light it, thinks the daughter at the end
of *Sunlit Soufflé* because her father has
returned from death
as an acrobat performing
in the moon-dipped yard.
I too have felt the strangeness
of having a mouth, a body,
the air sticking to its ribs,
of simply walking the breathy dark.
Spill out light, like water
into palm, I thought, in the balcony
of theater four, where
Rachmaninov's yellow flowers
bloomed and wilted in my ears,
where you taught me snow,
and luck from fate, and how when one is twenty
one should be drunk always
and running through the crowded streets.

Where you taught me décolleté, and Gauloises,
how I could write voluminously
about my love for the violinist
but that I'd lose my left green eye
and my night-job at the swank hotel.
You taught me love's an awful thing,
it makes a swimming bird of us,
that time is just the pocket watch
tied to a bottle rocket
in *Benedict and Julia*. You taught me masculine
and feminine interpretations
of pitch and woo. Oh you gods of French cinema
snoozing in a snowy field
of stars, I heard everything you had to say,
I listened when you told me how
to feel caressed by all of it,
like the girls who pin their hair in buns
shaped like croissants and walk along
the Seine in *Sentiments of a Life,*
who could at any moment lift
into the heavy air propelled by beauty.
And thank you for that scene, Moreau,
in *The Edge of Fire* where the dying man walks
into the ocean so he can wear it one last time,
and underneath the pier
he hears the children playing,
their voices washing up with seagull squawk
while one girl shows another
how to braid like lives

two ropes of hair into one. I listened
when you said
the mind just wants to shine it all right back,
that everything lives inside everything
as music, like in Tremeau's *The Sculptors*,
when the whole town learns to carve a little joy
from blocks of wood that have been speaking
to them in dreams. It's some great war
and when the whole town burns,
it burns faster than the burning center
of the earth, faster than its curling corners
fling their ash into the blue
that's stretching out, dropping down
along its way
a jewel in every eye.

Elizabeth Langemak

An Apology

Even young I knew:
imagination was mainly
for seeing how things would

not be. I practiced
on my dog. I imagined him
hit by a car, frozen, fallen

into a permanent sleep.
When he developed a cancerous limp
instead, I understood nothing

I could think of would be
as I thought. I moved on
to bigger things, worked

on technique: twenty thoughts
on college roommates,
thirty guesses about where I might live,

how I might meet my husband.
Each came to me unexpected,
as I could not have foreseen them.

I wouldn't have wanted to know
and so I thought harder, I imagined
my work, my friends, the ways

I thought I could love people. It was good
not to glimpse these: they were
not blurry nor dim but totally out

my range, they did not shock
nor startle but each as it happened
let itself in, a stranger with a key

to the room where I waited. For pleasure,
I tried small things too: the color
of my first car, how good I would be

at racquetball, if dinner would taste
like the picture made it smell.
None were as I thought. After a while

surprise no longer surprised me;
I knew I could not even say what I felt
when I practiced beforehand. When

I met you, I looked for each word I wanted
to speak and when it was not there
I was not amazed because by then

I knew imagination was a machine
for not knowing. All of this is to say
that last night when you said

I was not thinking of you
when I thought of us I said, *I think
of you always*, but I see now

how I have actually imagined
everything else. Sometimes I think
of what we might be instead. I know

I am not quite what I thought,
that I cannot say well
what I most want to say.

You are not what I expected
either. Forgive me for imagining
you otherwise.

Erin Hoover

On the Origin of Species

What if the pilled arms of waiting room chairs
in a fertility clinic are the closest I come
to natural selection now, the date of my last
period hard and fast as my account balance,
this perpetual withdrawing of eggs? When I said

I wanted this—coughed out in some exam room,
I want a baby, as if by saying it, someone else
would have to deal with that—the doctor
asked if I'd ever thought about *just having sex*.
As in, maybe you find a decent man and forget

the condom, maybe you say you're on the pill,
and then you do everything on your own,
like always. Instead I'm on Park Avenue
to see how many eggs I have left. As it turns out,
a lot—grayscale caviar on an ultrasound screen,

but soaking in their nightly bath of white wine,
I should be paid not to harvest them. Quick math,
how long must I quit drinking, starting
when? As if it could be entered on any chart
that while everybody gets lit in the other room,

I watch the drug dealer's toddler, wiping up spit,
reading to her out of a dingy picture book.
Or maybe my balance is better articulated
this way: the nine-to-five mill where I've chunked
a penny pile of hours can have my baby's

nonexistent fat calves, the litany of boyfriends
who flickered off lay claim to its paunch,
but its face? Let it be the times I kissed a bottle
with my unslakeable mouth. Maybe a woman
can only be classified as two of three things,

take-no-prisoners striver, stroller maven,
or sad sack, sailing into the party with her skirt
on backwards and heart dangerously close
to finally torching its own cavity, save
this continuance, of I know not what, or how.

Corrie Lynn White

Gravy

If I keep digging under
the driver's seat, I'll find one
more quarter so I can park.
Or a tampon. A bottle of water.
That old sound of sloshing
at stop lights. When I first met you,
I'd sit straight in your truck
and tell myself *It's just lunch.*
It was just chicken salad
on croissants, dining outside
on plastic tables. I'd watch
you while we drove on Capital
Boulevard past the Denture
Makers, Sally's Adult Video,
Raleigh Tire and U-Haul.
You knew where you were going.
And the world was flat on its back—
reaching like hell to flip us on ours,
make us stare up and forget
what we ate, the underwear
we had on. My favorite ones
I'd accidentally swept under
the bed four months ago.
That's simply where they had gone.

I thought the world wanted me
to keep stirring the gravy around
with a wooden spoon, because
as soon as I looked away, the gravy
would boil over. The world said
give the spoon to someone else.
So we watch the birds fly over Wells
Fargo. It's hard to believe
they get up that far.

Debbie Benson

Memory
\ *měm'ə-rē* \

1
Permission to recount a narrative series;
                              History of encounters encircling
                                          the self as though spool
or spell; Device through which one's anger betrays a sociocultural contracted silence

2
Turntable vision surrounding imperfection
                              preceding any finite ending,
i.e. death; Quality of regret in which one yearns to return, deny,
                              or destroy that which is subsequent to loss

3
Capacity for psychic reenactment
                              of past possibilities actualized; Disabled present
            with the availability of specters

4
Head-shaped briefcase, with protectiveness
                              of sense; Discernment of a value
        through comparison of tense

5
Christmas bulbs that hotly sink the branches of the pine;
                    Large as planets, pawed by cats, red
                                        and purple heavy glass
glows, pieces strung by thread-thin lightning quickly furnished, globe
                                                    to globe

6
Worry for the future, with refusal to change
                one's clothes; Grandiose catatonia, i.e., that clocks
                                        are hoped to freeze
in cooperation with personal inertia

7
Quality of being chased, accessed across nets
                                    of former telegraph; Preoccupation
                    with hands with mercy with
            ands; Rips in the Kansas kitchen curtain, flapping anyway in storm

8
Sequence, accumulation of nights; Stacks
                of city homes daily darkening uner the shadow of a giant,
                                black wing; So the light
from our lamps uprises in rings, from all tables and dressers
                            and bedside boards, to blight the dim
                                        of other things

Michael Boccardo

What No One Told Me About Autumn

Why it boils over without apology. Why
lawns lining every home erupt

in the night, fevered by some unnamable sorrow.
Why the sky hides so often, a blister

I've fingered since childhood.
When it uses words like mercy

and regret, I lose myself in the backyard
the way a match loses its grip on the dark.

Here, between two pines, I might hear
what was once the gossip of sheets

my mother snapped against a line,
father's shirts pinned shoulder

to shoulder, collars flared, buttons with nothing
to clutch. I think of the crickets who will later spark

the air with their duplicitous refrain,
how I will follow them, barefoot,

moss dusting my heels. And for what?
Tell me that if I look back now,

I won't see how each grief solders us
to the next: a house clapped shut,

gagged, leaning into its hollowed bones.
Leaves, battered by wind, seized

between the tines of an abandoned rake.
Their ceaseless falling. How they wait

and wait to become tinder, then smoke,
then ash. How I cannot change it.

Elsbeth Pancrazi

What's penciled in

your heart

the ocean steps up
to erase

Its keyhole
is stolen

the key insists
with a beep

I open

my amnesia capsule
in champagne

On our honeymoon
I'm going to

forever first

Jade Ramsey

She Lives in a Pat of Butter

It isn't what she'd intended but she really has no choice—the miniscule woman named Dione with long black hair. The Ivory Tusk from Sherwin Williams (which glows in her mother-in-law's kitchen beautifully) wasn't mixed properly and the walls that she dreamed of are now melting—there is too much Sunshine or Lemon or Jaundice—margarine drips on the couch with that smell of old toast from the Waffle House. She recalls the ceramic that hung by her mother's stove when she was a child: *Everything is better with butter and love.* But this much love makes her staircase slippery and her own children fall. They stop asking friends over. And her husband returns to the bottle. Dione stops washing her hair. The headboard is too close to the wall: her pillow is yellowed. And she sleeps alone. She is shaving her head. Her skin is oiled like the creases of Bundt pans, ready for heat, the oven of her mother-in-law.

Angela Voras-Hills

Preserving

I can spend a whole winter
        in the summer of these lemons
                if they're covered in enough salt.

                Trucks are salting the roads
        so I can drive. Men
salt the earth so I can walk

without falling. When I fall,
        I catch myself with my face.
                When I fall, I go

                to the hospital, to make sure
        the baby is still alive.
There are so many small things

to worry about in a large way.
        How much coffee should I drink?
                For every bean ground, someone

                is having sex or a child
        is starving. How do I know?
Because I'm always reading

warning labels or watching
      children pick dandelions near the slide.
          Except they are never

dandelions, but toads. And the children
      pick them up and throw them
          into the pond by the handful,

      believing they are frogs.
   And we can't blame them for not knowing
what swims, what sinks, what floats.

Kenny Tanemura

Expulsion

Because he said *chink*
I said *wetback*
not knowing

the impact any more
than him
skin glistening

a crack in the wall
where circus performers
dangle from ropes

on the other side.
A back you can't see
but only feel

the dew there, a hole
in the fence
dividing two families

both unhappy.
Happily as fences do,
tilting at crazy

angles no one
can graze. Ricochet.
How a bullet

bounced, found its way
into a baby's neck,
the velocity slowed

by the expulsion enough
to keep the baby alive.
Not the language

of race but expulsion,
the way a bullet glances,
looks and looks

Aran Donovan

two left feet

I cannot be danced,
not, certainly, led,
not foxtrotted, conned,
not fixed. I haven't
the shoes. Once, pelt
ruined, a dead fox lay
roadside. Footless, for
I never saw it run.
I hadn't the shoes
to lend it, moonless
and mindstunned. Return
to my empty window worse
than begun.
Own waltz, own trolley,
ding dong. The right
steps and I'm gone. Good
as useless, these shoes.
Black nights come
for everyone.

Micah Chatterton

Now, Someday

We came through here once, past
chains of rock-scarred, selfsame hills, past
the dusty squares that suddenly turn
to green lettuce like bottleglass, and back,
past yellowing honkytonks, taquerias, past
so many sheep huddled onto planks
of shade under a billboard.
"I'm going to be a writer someday,"
Ezra said, "but not as my main job."
I was taking him up the mountain
to a camp for children with cancer
and other catastrophic ailments, a week
of wallet-making and pine cones, trees
shifting. Between his ankles, his backpack
flapped back, unzipped like always,
to show an empty drawing pad
and a spray of unwritten letters, one
for each day, envelopes stamped
and addressed home.
Sailing his hand out onto the 74,
I asked him to name five amazing things
he hoped to do that week, the longest,
farthest we'd ever been apart.

What I remember now, is Ezra
wanted to swim. He wanted to see other
kids carved from the same soft wood
as him, to float up in that stinging cool
and count the swaddled PICC lines,
the shaved heads and heads
furred with post-chemo lanugo,
steroid plumped cheeks or ribs
thinned to stacking stones by nausea,
tattooed radiation crosses,
white, half-knitted surgical lines,
and then, then, the whip welts,
blue stretch marks fanning across
all their trunks and limbs.

What I remember now, is Ezra
being sent to the hospital the next day,
protocol for when his temperature tipped
over a hundred. I could hear him laughing
like always as I shuffled through
those shoe-smoothed, dustless hallways,
those hiss-shut doors. I could hear him
telling his nurses a dog and cat story
he'd written, or was going to write,
or imagined just that second.

What I remember now, is Ezra
dry drowning in my arms.

Courtney Kampa

Ars Biologica

Forgive me, for forgiving her,
your birth mother. I am unforgiving
unless for selfish reasons, and it seems my reasons
are as selfish as they come. I am trying
to say that I am thankful
for your grief—thankful, at least, that it keeps you
here, where, daily, your cheekbones bend a little higher
toward the stuff Mongolian bridges
were inspired from, and little-woman, or
soon-woman, I can feel you growing
through our floorboards: bones lengthening
in your torso, skin whipped by an upwind gust
of prepubescence and today I bought three bottles
of nail polish you'll like from CVS, hues
called Not Really A Waitress, Plasma, and If You've Got It,
Haunt It, and, though I mostly bought the last one
for myself, I bought all three for
you in reparation for last week's purchase, Miso Happy
With This Color, which I painted on your toes
and still feel bad about. You know by now
not all of us are Irish. I know by now you knew all along
why Aunt Donna gave you Asian Barbie dolls
for Christmas; why, when you asked mom
buckling your car seat Did I come out

of your tummy? she said, Grace you came straight from
my heart and then got really
quiet. According to your recent Google history
there are lots of questions you aren't asking
and that's probably my fault
since you don't ask questions the same way I don't
when I know I won't know how exactly
to respond, and all of us learn exactly
by example. For example, the drugstore cashier on 106th
is from a town three miles from your own
and all I ever say is wave goodbye.
Or that, with only sisters, I don't know
how to talk about a brother—yours. He's probably
with her right now—closing
their front door shut to the cold; turning soap
in his hands. Keep Him Around is a purplish polish
I used on you last month, your sticky palms
quiet on my knees, your fingernails shaped differently
than mine, the family rosary going on and on
around us. This family, like an afterworld.
Our Lady of Loss. Our Lady of Is-There-Something-Fixable-
Inside-Us. I can't see your mother but I can see you
hate yourself for wanting her. Forgive me
for forgiving her for giving
you away. Mothers are never a metaphor
for something else. Our Lady of Teach-Us-That-Having-Been-Loved-Badly-
Is-Not-the-Same-As-Being-Unloved.
Our Lady of Not-Asking-Why. The broken heart has need
for other hearts broken differently, but
one sister in ruin ruins the other sisters

identically. There are days when your footsteps
out our kitchen and up the stairs carry you to places
I can't find you. Nights when the outline
your body, peach-hot, fevers into your sheets
looks nothing like your own. The past should go away
but never does. It bangs inside us like an
extra heart, though it is not. It is not at all like that.

Contributors' Notes

MELISSA BARRETT is the recipient of an Ohio Arts Council Individual Excellence Award for poetry. Her poems have appeared or are forthcoming in *Narrative, Gulf Coast, Kenyon Review Online, Anti-,* and *Web Conjunctions*. She teaches at the award-winning urban middle school Columbus Collegiate Academy in Columbus, Ohio.

DEBBIE BENSON is completing her doctorate in clinical psychology from Yeshiva University, and currently works in a state psychiatric hospital. Her poems have appeared or are forthcoming in *The Cape Rock, Barrow Street, LIT, CROWD, elimae,* and other journals. Her awards include the Ann Stanford Poetry Prize from *Southern California Review* and the 2013 Vern Cowles Prize for a Trinity of Poems from Southeast Missouri State University Press. She lives in New York City with her husband, Hill Krishnan.

MICHAEL BOCCARDO's work has been published in various journals, including *Kestrel, The Southern Review, Prairie Schooner,* and *The Journal,* as well as the anthology *Spaces Between Us: Poetry, Prose, and Art on HIV/AIDS*. He is a multiple recipient of the Dorothy Sargent Rosenberg Poetry Prize, and serves as assistant editor for *Cave Wall*. He lives with his partner in High Point, North Carolina, where he is currently working on his first collection.

MICHELLE BONCZEK is the author of the chapbook *The Art of the Nipple* (Orange Monkey, 2013) and an editor at *The Poet's Billow* (thepoetsbillow. org). Her poems have appeared in over 60 literary journals and magazines including *cream city review, Crazyhorse, Green Mountains Review, Orion,*

Water-Stone Review, and *Weber Contemporary West*. She holds a PhD from Western Michigan University, an MFA from Eastern Washington University, and currently teaches at the SUNY College of Environmental Science and Forestry in Syracuse, New York.

CLAUDIA BURBANK is a graduate of Vassar College and pursued her MBA at New York University. Her honors include the *Poets & Writers* Maureen Egen Writers Exchange Award, fellowships from the New Jersey State Council on the Arts and the Jentel Artist Residency, the Inkwell Prize (judged by Alice Quinn), and several Pushcart Prize nominations. In addition, she was a finalist for the Center for Book Arts competition, the Beulah Rose Award. Her work has been featured on *Verse Daily* and the *Best American Poetry* and *Poets & Writers* websites. Her poetry and fiction can be found in such journals as *The Antioch Review, Washington Square Review, Prairie Schooner, upstreet, Subtropics*, and *cream city review*.

MICAH CHATTERTON earned an MFA in Creative Writing and Writing for the Performing Arts from the University of California, Riverside, and now works, with gusto, as an elementary school librarian. His work has appeared or is forthcoming in *The Coachella Review, Kindred Magazine*, and *Atticus Review*, and is anthologized in *The Cancer Poetry Project 2* (Tasora Books, 2013). He lives and writes in the Inland Empire of Southern California.

DARIN CICCOTELLI has published poems in *Fence, Hayden's Ferry Review, Kenyon Review, VOLT*, and *ZYZZYVA*. He received his MFA from the Michener Center for Writers and his PhD from the University of Houston, where he was the managing editor of *Gulf Coast: A Journal of Literature and Fine Art*. He currently teaches at Soka University of America.

MEG DAY is a 2013 recipient of an NEA Literature Fellowship in Poetry and the author of *When All You Have Is a Hammer* (winner of the 2012 Gertrude Press Chapbook Contest) and *We Can't Read This* (winner of the 2013 Gazing Grain Chapbook Contest). A 2012 AWP Intro Journals Award winner, she has also received awards and fellowships from the Lambda Literary Foundation, Hedgebrook, Squaw Valley Writers, and the International Queer Arts Festival. Meg is currently a PhD fellow in poetry and disability poetics at the University of Utah.

ARAN DONOVAN lives in the charming squalor of New Orleans. Once, she wanted to be a paleontologist. Her poetry has appeared in the journals *RHINO, New Ohio Review*, and *Southern Poetry Review*, among others.

TARFIA FAIZULLAH is the author of *Seam* (Southern Illinois University Press, 2014). Her poems have appeared in *Ninth Letter, New England Review, Ploughshares, The Missouri Review*, and elsewhere. A Kundiman fellow, she received her MFA in poetry from Virginia Commonwealth University. She is the recipient of a Fulbright fellowship, a Dorothy Sargent Rosenberg award, a Ploughshares Cohen Award, scholarships from Bread Loaf Writers' Conference and Sewanee Writers' Conference, fellowships from Kenyon Review Writers' Workshop and Vermont Studio Center, and other honors.

JENNIFER GIVHAN was a Pen Rosenthal Emerging Voices Fellow, as well as the *DASH* 2013 Poetry Prize winner, a St. Lawrence Book Award finalist, and a Vernice Quebodeaux Pathways finalist for her poetry collection. She attends the MFA program at Warren Wilson College, and her work has appeared in over 50 literary journals, including *Prairie Schooner, Indiana Review, Rattle, Cutthroat*, and *The Los Angeles Review*. She teaches composition at Western New Mexico University. You can visit her online at *jennifergivhan.com*.

ANDREW C. GOTTLIEB lives and writes in Irvine, California, but spends much of his time in Seattle, Washington. He is the reviews editor for *Terrain. org*, and his work has appeared in many journals including the *American Literary Review, Bellevue Literary Review, Beloit Fiction Journal, Ecotone, ISLE, Provincetown Arts, Poets & Writers, Salon.com*, and *Tampa Review*. In 2005, his chapbook of poems, *Halflives*, was published by New Michigan Press.

MIKKO HARVEY is a student in the MFA program for poetry at Ohio State University. He is also a graduate of Vassar College, where he won the Academy of American Poets Prize. His poems appear in journals such as the *New Haven Review, Coconut, Birdfeast, PANK*, and *Juked*.

ANNA CLAIRE HODGE is a second year PhD student at Florida State University. She received her MFA from Virginia Commonwealth University. Her work has appeared in *Copper Nickel, Hayden's Ferry Review, Bellingham Review, The Collagist*, and *The Journal*, among others. Her poems were chosen as finalists for both the *Copper Nickel* Poetry Contest and the 49th Parallel Award for Poetry.

ANNA MARIA HONG is the 2013-14 Visiting Creative Writer at Ursinus College and was the 2010-11 Bunting Fellow in Poetry at the Radcliffe Institute for Advanced Study. The recipient of *Poetry* magazine's 2013 Frederick Bock Prize, she has published poems in numerous journals and anthologies including *Green Mountains Review, Southwest Review, Beloit Poetry Journal, Fairy Tale Review, Fence, POOL, jubilat, Mandorla, Unsplendid, Boston Review, 250 Poems: A Portable Anthology*, and *The Best American Poetry 2013*.

ERIN HOOVER is a PhD student in Florida State University's Creative Writing Program, where she is assistant editor of *The Southeast Review* and volunteers for VIDA: Women in Literary Arts. She has poems published or forthcoming in *Prairie Schooner, Gargoyle, Lunch Ticket, Mason's Road, Spry*, and elsewhere.

ROCHELLE HURT is the author of a novel in poems, *The Rusted City*, forthcoming in the Marie Alexander Series from White Pine Press (2014). Her work has been published in *Mid-American Review, Cincinnati Review, The Collagist, Meridian, Versal,* and elsewhere. She lives in Cincinnati, Ohio.

JOHN JAMES holds an MFA in poetry from Columbia University, where he received an Academy of American Poets Prize. His work has appeared or is forthcoming in *Boston Review, The Kenyon Review, DIAGRAM, Hayden's Ferry Review, Washington Square, Sixth Finch,* and elsewhere. He teaches at Bellarmine University in Louisville, Kentucky, where he co-curates the Speak Social Reading Series.

JOSH KALSCHEUR is the author of one collection of poetry, *Tidal* (forthcoming from Four Way Books), which won the 2013 Four Way Books Levis Prize in Poetry. His poetry has appeared in or is forthcoming from *Boston Review, Slate, The Iowa Review,* and *jubilat,* among others. He currently lives in Madison, Wisconsin.

COURTNEY KAMPA's work has appeared in *Boston Review, Colorado Review, TriQuarterly, The Journal, The National Poetry Review, New England Review,* and elsewhere, and has received awards and distinctions from *Poets & Writers Magazine, The Atlantic,* and *North American Review.* She holds an MFA from Columbia and works at a publishing house in New York.

ELIZABETH LANGEMAK lives in Philadelphia, Pennsylvania.

SARAH LEVINE is from outside Boston, Massachusetts. She received her MFA in poetry from Sarah Lawrence College and her BA in English from the University of Massachusetts Amherst's Commonwealth Honors College. Her work has appeared or is forthcoming in *PANK, Vinyl,* and *Handsome,* among others. She won *Westchester Review*'s Writers' Under 30 Poetry Contest, has been nominated for a Pushcart Prize, and is the poetry editor for *Boiler Journal*. *Her Man*, her first chapbook, will be released from The New Megaphone Press in 2014.

JASON MACEY is a poet and teacher living and working in northeast Pennsylvania. When he's not reading, writing, or teaching, Jason is running absurdly long distances to train for his next marathon.

LO KWA MEI-EN's poems have appeared in *Boston Review, Guernica, The Kenyon Review, West Branch*, and other journals, and won the *Crazyhorse* Lynda Hull Memorial Poetry Prize and the *Gulf Coast* Poetry Prize. Her first book, *Yearling*, won the 2013 Kundiman Poetry Prize and is forthcoming from Alice James Books. A graduate of Ohio State University's MFA Program, she ventures out from and returns to Ohio.

SCOTT MILES is from Atlanta, Georgia, and is currently an MFA candidate at Indiana University. His areas of interest include featural alphabets, abstract expressionism, and Gucci Mane.

PETER MISHLER was educated at Emerson College and Syracuse University. He teaches public school in Central New York. His poems have appeared in *Crazyhorse, Ninth Letter*, and other journals.

GLORIA MUÑOZ holds a BA from Sarah Lawrence College and an MFA from the University of South Florida. She has been honored by the Estelle J. Zbar Poetry Prize, the Bettye Newman Poetry Award, the New York Summer Writer's Institute Fellowship, and the Think Small to Think Big Artist Grant. Her work has appeared in *Acentos Review, Dark Phrases, The Brooklyn Review, The Sarah Lawrence Review, Sweet Lit* and other print and online publications. She is currently pursuing a PhD in literacy studies and working to complete her first book of poetry and translation.

LISA ALLEN ORTIZ was born and raised in the far reaches of Northern California. Her poems have appeared in *ZYZZYVA, The Literary Review, Crab Creek Review*, and others. Two chapbooks of her poems are available: *Turns Out* from Main Street Rag Publishing and *Self Portrait as a Clock* from Finishing Line Press. She currently lives with her husband and two daughters in Cusco, Peru.

ELSBETH PANCRAZI studied poetry at Vassar College and at New York University. She was a 2013 Poets House Fellow and artist-in-residence at Caldera Arts in Sisters, Oregon. Her poems have appeared in *Forklift, Ohio; H_ngm_n; No, Dear;* and *Paperbag.*

HANNAH SANGHEE PARK has received fellowships and awards from The MacDowell Colony, the Fulbright Program, 4Culture, the Iowa Arts Council/ National Endowment for the Arts, and elsewhere. She holds a BA from the University of Washington (2008) and an MFA from the Iowa Writers' Workshop (2010). Her chapbook *Ode Days Ode* was published through The Catenary Press. She was recently named a 2013 Ruth Lilly Poetry Fellowship recipient, and currently studies in the Writing for Screen & Television Program at the USC School of Cinematic Arts.

LAURA PASSIN is a writer, professor, and feminist at large. She holds a PhD from Northwestern and an MFA from the University of Oregon. Her poetry has recently appeared or is forthcoming in *Prairie Schooner, Bellevue Literary Review*, and *Adrienne: A Poetry Journal of Queer Women.* Laura lives in Chicagoland with her partner, two cats, and way too many books.

JADE RAMSEY is an associate editor for *Gingerbread House Magazine.* Her works can be found in *Blue Lyra, Goblin Fruit*, the anthology of fairy tale poetry *On the Dark Path, Rubbertop Review, Ayris, Stone Highway Review, Ancient Paths*, and many others. She lives in Tallahassee, Florida with her fiancé.

KYEREN REGEHR holds an MFA in Creative Writing (University of Victoria) and serves on the poetry board of *The Malahat Review*. She received a 2013 grant from Canada Council of the Arts to finish her first poetry collection *Cult Life*—the title poem was longlisted for the 2012 CBC Literary Awards. Her work has appeared in Canadian and Australian literary journals and anthologies such as *The Fiddlehead, Grain, Prairie Fire, PRISM international, Room, Hecate, Poems from Planet Earth*, and is forthcoming in *The Antigonish Review, Filling Station*, and *The Literary Review of Canada*.

STEPHANIE ROGERS grew up in Middletown, Ohio, one of America's top ten fastest dying towns, according to *Forbes Magazine*. She completed her MA in English and comparative literature in 2005 from the University of Cincinnati, and in 2007, she received her MFA in poetry from the University of North Carolina at Greensboro. Her poetry has also appeared in journals such as *Southern Review, Pleiades*, and *Third Coast*, among others. Her feminist commentary has been published online at *Women and Hollywood, Ms. Magazine, Shakesville*, and *The Good Men Project*. She lives in a very tiny studio apartment in Brooklyn where she edits and writes for *Bitch Flicks*, a feminist media website she cofounded with Amber Leab in 2008.

JUSTIN RUNGE lives in Lawrence, Kansas, where he serves as poetry editor of *Parcel*. He is the author of two chapbooks, *Plainsight* (New Michigan Press, 2012) and *Hum Decode* (forthcoming from Greying Ghost Press). Poems of his have appeared in *Linebreak, DIAGRAM, Harpur Palate*, and elsewhere. He can be found at *justinrunge.me*.

MEIGHAN L. SHARP's work was included previously in *Best New Poets 2010*. She is a graduate of Linfield College and earned her MFA from the Jackson Center for Creative Writing at Hollins University. Her recent work appears in *Crazyhorse, Plume, Cimarron Review, The Florida Review*, and *DIALOGIST*.

She writes from Roanoke, Virginia, where her husband and son and a stalwart band of neighborhood kids provide many opportunities to abandon her work for a game of capture the flag.

MICHAEL SIMON is an editor in New York, where he is working on his first collection of poems. His poetry and prose have appeared in *Atlas Review, Cimarron Review, Denver Quarterly, Epiphany*, and elsewhere.

MAX SOMERS lives and works in the Midwest with his girlfriend, poet Sara Gelston. In 2012, he won the Robinson Jeffers Tor House Poetry Award and was runner-up for the "Discovery"/*Boston Review* Poetry Prize. Recent work appears in *Hayden's Ferry Review, Prairie Schooner, Third Coast, Fugue*, and *Puerto Del Sol*. Every August he races a vintage motorcycle at the Bonneville Salt Flats.

BENJAMIN SUTTON is the author of the chapbook *Then, the Unabridged*, forthcoming in *Black Warrior Review*. His poetry recently won the Kay Murphy Prize from the University of New Orleans and *Bayou Magazine*, judged by Dawn Lundy Martin. Other poems have recently appeared or are forthcoming in *The Literary Review, Redivider, Sycamore Review, Salt Hill*, and *Third Coast*, among others.

L.J. SYSKO holds an MFA in poetry from New England College. She has been the recipient of an Emerging Artist Grant from Delaware Division of the Arts. Other awards include the Academy of American Poets' Jean Corrie Prize, Lafayette College's H. MacKnight Black Prize, and three awards from the Dorothy Sargent Rosenberg Memorial Foundation. She has had work published in *Ploughshares, New York Quarterly, Rattle, 5am*, and other journals. Sysko is chair of the Tower Hill School English Department in Wilmington, Delaware where she lives with her husband and two children. For more information, visit *ljsysko.com*.

KENNY TANEMURA has an MFA from Purdue University. He lives and works in the San Francisco Bay Area, tutoring English to international engineers and designers in Silicon Valley. He is currently working on a book of poems about Japan and Japanese Americans.

CHAD TEMPLES lives and works in Raleigh, North Carolina.

BRIAN TIERNEY's poems have appeared in, or are forthcoming in, *The Kenyon Review, Hayden's Ferry Review, Caliban, Poetry Quarterly*, and others. A small body of his work was awarded first runner-up in the *Ploughshares* 2013 Emerging Writer's Contest. He earned an MFA in poetry from Bennington College, and lives in Pittsburgh.

EMILY VAN KLEY's fiction and poetry have received several awards and honorable mentions, including the 2009 *Florida Review* Editor's Prize and the 2011 *Iowa Review* Award. Her work also appears in the newly released anthology *The Way North: Collected Upper Michigan New Works* from Wayne State University Press. She currently lives in Olympia with her partner and a belligerent cockapoo named Fancypants.

ANGELA VORAS-HILLS earned her MFA at UMass-Boston and was a fellow at the Writers' Room of Boston. Her work has appeared or is forthcoming in *Kenyon Review Online, Hayden's Ferry Review*, and *Linebreak*, among others. Her first full-length manuscript was recently a finalist for Milkweed Editions' Lindquist & Vennum Prize in Poetry. She currently lives in Madison, Wisconsin.

CORRIE LYNN WHITE's poems are forthcoming in *The Greensboro Review* and *Grist: The Journal for Writers*. Originally from North Carolina, she holds an MFA from UNC Greensboro where she currently teaches English. In 2013, she received the Noel Callow Poetry Prize, sponsored by the Academy of American Poets.

A student of America's shorthand history, **DEREK JG WILLIAMS** grew up studying comic books and the backs of baseball cards. He's an MFA candidate at UMass Boston and recent runner up for *Knockout Literary Journal's* Reginald Shepherd Poetry Prize. His poems are published or forthcoming in the *Bellingham Review, Main Street Rag, The Quotable, RHINO, Knockout,* and *Palooka Literary Journal,* among others. Derek's a proponent of handclaps in songs and needs no excuse to celebrate all the time, anytime.

CORI A. WINROCK's poems have appeared in (or are waiting in the wings of) *Anti-, Black Warrior Review, Colorado Review, Denver Quarterly, From the Fishouse,* and elsewhere. She won the 2012 SLS-*St. Petersburg Review* Award and was a semi-finalist for the Discovery/*Boston Review* Poetry Contest. Her manuscript has been a finalist for a number of prizes, including the Walt Whitman Award. Her first book, *This Coalition of Bones,* is forthcoming from Kore Press in early 2014. She is currently a visiting assistant professor at SUNY Geneseo.

AMY WOOLARD serves as senior policy attorney for Voices for Virginia's Children, a policy research and advocacy non-profit, working on child welfare, foster care, juvenile justice, and child poverty issues. She is a graduate of the Iowa Writers' Workshop and the University of Virginia School of Law. In addition to *Smartish Pace*, her work has appeared or is forthcoming in the *Virginia Quarterly Review, the Massachusetts Review, Fence, The Journal,* and *Crazyhorse,* among others. She lives in Charlottesville, Virginia.

JAVIER ZAMORA was born in La Herradura, La Paz, El Salvador. At the age of nine he immigrated to the "Yunaited Estais." His chapbook, *Nine Immigrant*

Years, is the winner of the 2011 Organic Weapon Arts Contest. Zamora is a CantoMundo fellow and a Bread Loaf work-study scholarship recipient. He has received scholarships from Frost Place, Napa Valley, Squaw Valley, and VONA. His poems appear or are forthcoming in *Interrupture, NewBorder, Ostrich Review, Ploughshares, Poet Lore,* among others.

Acknowledgments

Claudia Burbank's "TGIF" was previously published in *The Antioch Review*.

Meg Day's "Taker of the Temperature, Keeper of the Hope Chest" was previously published in *Adrienne*.

Aran Donovan's "two left feet" was previously published in *Rattle*.

Tarfia Faizullah's "Self-Portrait as Slinky" was previously published in *Ninth Letter*.

Jennifer Givhan's "Karaoke Night at the Asylum" was previously published in *Indiana Review*.

Mikko Harvey's "Cannonball" was previously published in *Juked*.

Anna Claire Hodge's "Where We Have No Business" was previously published in *Copper Nickel*.

Anna Maria Hong's "Four Barrels, Jaw & Locket" was previously published in *Unsplendid* and *Verse Daily*.

Erin Hoover's "On the Origin of Species" is forthcoming in *Gargoyle*.

Rochelle Hurt's "Poem in Which I Play the Runaway" was previously published in *The Collagist*.

Josh Kalscheur's "Katari" was previously published in *The Iowa Review*.

Courtney Kampa's "Ars Biologica" was previously published in *TriQuarterly*.

Elizabeth Langemak's "An Apology" was previously published in *C4*.

Lo Kwa Mei-en's "Romance in Which Open Season Changes Everything" was previously published in *APARTMENT Poetry*.

Hannah Sanghee Park's "BANG" was previously published in *32 Poems*.

Jade Ramsey's "She Lives in a Pat of Butter" was previously published in *Gargoyle*.

Kyeren Regehr's "Eversion" was previously published in *Prairie Fire*.

Justin Runge's "History" was previously published in *Rattle*.

Meighan L. Sharp's "Beyond Measure" was previously published in *DIALOGIST*.

Derek JG Williams's "Ode to the Tongue" was previously published in *Knockout Literary Magazine*.

Cori A. Winrock's "Débridement" was previously published in *Versal*.

Amy Woolard's "A Girl Gets Sick of a Rose" was previously published in *Smartish Pace*.

Participating Magazines

32 Poems
32poems.com

The Adroit Journal
adroit.co.nr

AGNI
bu.edu/agni

Alligator Juniper
prescott.edu/alligatorjuniper

Anti-
anti-poetry.com

Antioch Review
antiochreview.org

Apple Valley Review
applevalleyreview.com

Arsenic Lobster Poetry Journal
arseniclobster.magere.com

Bamboo Ridge
bambooridge.com

Bat City Review
batcityreview.la.utexas.edu

The Bear Deluxe Magazine
orlo.org

Bellevue Literary Review
blreview.org

Bellingham Review
bhreview.org

The Believer
believermag.com

Beloit Poetry Journal
bpj.org

Birmingham Poetry Review
birminghampoetryreview.org

The Bitter Oleander
bitteroleander.com

*Blackbird: an online journal of
literature and the arts*
blackbird.vcu.edu

BLOOM
artsinbloom.com

The Boiler Journal
theboilerjournal.com

BOOTH
booth.butler.edu

Boston Review
bostonreview.net

Boxcar Poetry Review
boxcarpoetry.com

Carolina Quarterly
cqonline.web.unc.edu

Cave Wall
cavewallpress.com

Cerise Press
cerisepress.com

Cincinnati Review
cincinnatireview.com

The Collagist
dzancbooks.org/thecollagist

The Common
thecommononline.org

Conte
conteonline.net

crazyhorse
crazyhorse.cofc.edu

Dappled Things
dappledthings.org

Devil's Lake
devilslakejournal.com

EVENT
eventmags.com

Fjords Review
fjordsreview.com

Flycatcher
flycatcherjournal.org

Free State Review
freestatereview.com

Georgia Review
garev.uga.edu

Gertrude
gertrudepress.org

The Greensboro Review
greensbororeview.org

Guernica Magazine
guernicamag.com

Gulf Coast
gulfcoastmag.org

Harvard Review
harvardreview.org

Hayden's Ferry Review
haydensferryreview.org

Hunger Mountain
hungermtn.org

Image
imagejournal.org

Indiana Review
indianareview.org

The Iowa Review
iowareview.uiowa.edu

The Journal
thejournalmag.org

Juked
juked.com

The Kenyon Review
kenyonreview.org

The Los Angeles Review
losangelesreview.org

The MacGuffin
schoolcraft.edu/macguffin

The Massachusetts Review
massreview.org

Memorious
memorious.org

Michigan Quarterly Review
michiganquarterlyreview.com

New England Review
nereview.com

New Orleans Review
neworleansreview.org

Nimrod International Journal
utulsa.edu/nimrod

Orion
orionmagazine.org

PANK
pankmagazine.com

The Paris-American
theparisamerican.com

The Pinch
thepinchjournal.com

Pleiades: A Journal of New Writing
ucmo.edu/pleiades

Prairie Schooner
prairieschooner.unl.edu

Raleigh Review
raleighreview.org

Rattle
rattle.com

Red Lightbulbs
redlightbulbs.net

River Styx
riverstyx.org

Room Magazine
roommagazine.com

Smartish Pace
smartishpace.com

So to Speak: a feminist journal of language and art
sotospeakjournal.org

The Southeast Review
southeastreview.org

Southern Humanities Review
cla.auburn.edu/shr

Southern Indiana Review
usi.edu/sir

The Southern Review
thesouthernreview.org

Southwest Review
smu.edu/southwestreview

Spillway
spillway.org

St. Petersburg Review
stpetersburgreview.com

Stirring: A Literary Collection
sundresspublications.com/stirring

Subtropics
english.ufl.edu/subtropics

Thrush Poetry Journal
thrushpoetryjournal.com

Toe Good Poetry
toegoodpoetry.com

The Tusculum Review
tusculum.edu/tusculumreview

Unsplendid
unsplendid.com

Verse Wisconsin
versewisconsin.org

Vinyl Poetry
vinylpoetry.com

Virginia Quarterly Review
vqronline.org

Waccamaw
waccamawjournal.com

Washington Square Review
washingtonsquarereview.com

Web Del Sol Review of Books
wdsreviewofbooks.webdelsol.com

Willow Springs
willowsprings.ewu.edu

Participating Writing Programs

92Y Unterberg Poetry Center Writing Program
New York, NY
92y.org/WritingProgram

American University MFA in Creative Writing
Washington, DC
american.edu/cas/literature/mfa

Ashland University MFA in Creative Writing
Ashland, OH
ashland.edu/cas/majors/master-fine-arts-creative-writing

Auburn University Creative Writing Program
Auburn, AL
cla.auburn.edu/english/graduate-studies/ma/concentration-in-creative-writing

Colorado State University MFA Program in Creative Writing
Fort Collins, CO
creativewriting.colostate.edu

Columbia College Chicago MFA in Creative Writing - Poetry
Chicago, IL
colum.edu/Academics/English_Department/Programs/poetry/MFA

Creative Writing at Florida State University
Tallahassee, FL
english.fsu.edu/crw

Earlham School of Religion's Ministry of Writing Program
Richmond, IN
esr.earlham.edu

Emerson College Creative Writing (MFA)
Boston, MA
emerson.edu/academics/departments/writing-literature-publishing/graduate-degrees/creative-writing

Fine Arts Work Center in Provincetown
Provincetown, MA
fawc.org

**George Mason University
Creative Writing**
Fairfax, VA
creativewriting.gmu.edu

**Hollins University Jackson Center
for Creative Writing**
Roanoke, VA
hollins.edu/jacksoncenter

Hunter College MFA Program
New York, NY
hunter.cuny.edu/creativewriting

The Iowa Writers' Workshop
Iowa City, IA
uiowa.edu/~iww

**Johns Hopkins University: The
Writing Seminars**
Baltimore, MD
writingseminars.jhu.edu

**Kansas State University MFA in
Creative Writing**
Manhattan, KS
k-state.edu/english/programs/cw

**Kennesaw State University MA in
Professional Writing Program**
Kennesaw, GA
ksu-mapw.com

Kundiman
New York, NY
kundiman.org

**McNeese State University MFA
Program in Creative Writing**
Lake Charles, LA
mfa.mcneese.edu

**Minnesota State University
Mankato MFA Program in
Creative Writing**
Mankato, MN
english.mnsu.edu/cw/cwmfa.html

**Monmouth University Department
of English**
West Long Branch, NJ
monmouth.edu/english.aspx

**Murray State University Low
Residency MFA Program**
Murray, KY
murraystate.edu/Academics/
CollegesDepartments/
CollegeOfHumanitiesAndFineArts/
EnglishAndPhilosophy/GraduatePrograms/
MFACreativeWriting.aspx

**New Mexico State University MFA
in Creative Writing**
Las Cruces, NM
english.nmsu.edu/mfa

New School Creative Writing
New York, NY
newschool.edu/public-engagement/mfa-creative-writing

North Carolina State University Creative Writing Program
Raleigh, NC
english.chass.ncsu.edu/creativewriting

Northwest Institute of Literary Arts Whidbey Writers Workshop
Freeland, WA
nila.edu/mfa

NYU Creative Writing Program
New York, NY
cwp.fas.nyu.edu/page/home

Ohio State Creative Writing Program
Columbus, OH
english.osu.edu/creative-writing-ohio-state-university

Pacific University Master of Fine Arts in Writing
Forest Grove, OR
pacificu.edu/as/mfa

San Diego State University Creative Writing Program
San Diego, CA
mfa.sdsu.edu

Sarah Lawrence College MFA Program
Bronxville, NY
slc.edu/graduate/programs/writing

Southeast Missouri State University MA in Professional Writing
Cape Girardeau, MO
semo.edu/english/study.htm

Southern Connecticut State University MFA Program in Creative Writing
New Haven, CT
southernct.edu/academics/schools/arts/departments/english/creativewriting/graduate

Texas Tech University Creative Writing Program
Lubbock, TX
english.ttu.edu

UCONN Creative Writing Program
Storrs, CT
creativewriting.uconn.edu

University of Alabama Creative Writing
Tuscaloosa, AL
english.ua.edu/grad/cw

University of Arkansas Programs in Creative Writing & Translation
Fayetteville, AR
mfa.uark.edu

University of British Columbia Creative Writing Program
Vancouver, BC, Canada
creativewriting.ubc.ca

University of Florida MFA Program in Creative Writing
Gainesville, FL
english.ufl.edu/crw

University of Idaho Creative Writing
Moscow, ID
uidaho.edu/class/english/mfacreativewriting

University of Illinois at Chicago Program for Writers
Chicago, IL
uic.edu/depts/engl/programs/grad_english/creative_writing

University of Kansas Creative Writing Program
Lawrence, KS
www2.ku.edu/~englishmfa

University of Massachusetts - Amherst MFA Program for Poets and Writers
Amherst, MA
umass.edu/english/MFA_home.htm

University of Massachusetts - Boston MFA Program in Creative Writing
Boston, MA
umb.edu/academics/cla/english/grad/mfa

University of Michigan Helen Zell Writers' Program
Ann Arbor, MI
lsa.umich.edu/english/grad/mfa

University of Mississippi MFA Program in English
University, MS
mfaenglish.olemiss.edu

University of Missouri Creative Writing Program
Columbia, MO
english.missouri.edu/creative-writing.html

University of Missouri - St. Louis MFA Program
St. Louis, MO
umsl.edu/~mfa

University of North Carolina at Greensboro MFA Writing Program
Greensboro, NC
mfagreensboro.org

University of North Dakota Department of English
Grand Forks, ND
arts-sciences.und.edu/english

University of North Texas Creative Writing Program
Denton, TX
english.unt.edu/creative-writing

University of Notre Dame Creative Writing Program
South Bend, IN
english.nd.edu/creative-writing

University of South Carolina MFA Program
Columbia, SC
artsandsciences.sc.edu/engl/grad/mfa

University of South Florida MFA in Creative Writing
Tampa, FL
english.usf.edu/graduate/concentrations/cw/degrees

University of Tennessee at Knoxville Creative Writing Program
Knoxville, TN
creativewriting.utk.edu

University of Texas Michener Center for Writers
Austin, TX
utexas.edu/academic/mcw

University of Wyoming MFA
Laramie, WY
uwyo.edu/creativewriting

Vermont College of Fine Arts MFA in Writing
Montpelier, VT
vcfa.edu/writing

Virginia Commonwealth University MFA in Creative Writing
Richmond, VA
has.vcu.edu/eng/graduate/mfa.htm

Virginia Tech MFA Program
Blacksburg, VA
graduate.english.vt.edu/MFA

West Virginia University Creative Writing Program
Morgantown, WV
creativewriting.wvu.edu

Western Michigan University
Creative Writing
Kalamazoo, MI
wmich.edu/english/creative-writing

BRENDA SHAUGHNESSY is an assistant professor of English at Rutgers-Newark University and Poetry Editor-at-Large at *Tin House*. She is the author of *Our Andromeda* (Copper Canyon, 2012), *Human Dark with Sugar* (Copper Canyon, 2008) and *Interior with Sudden Joy* (FSG, 2000). Her poetry has appeared in *Harper's*, *McSweeney's*, *The Nation*, *The New Yorker*, *The Paris Review* and elsewhere.

JAZZY DANZIGER is the author of *Darkroom* (University of Wisconsin, 2012), winner of the Brittingham Prize in Poetry. She lives and works in St. Louis, Missouri and can be visited online at jazzydanziger.com.